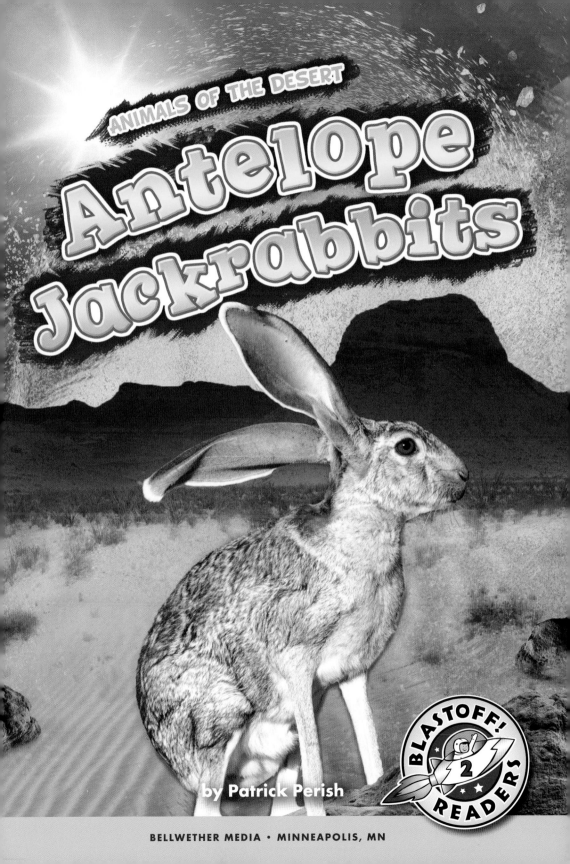

ANIMALS OF THE DESERT

Antelope Jackrabbits

by Patrick Perish

BLASTOFF! READERS
2

BELLWETHER MEDIA • MINNEAPOLIS, MN

Blastoff! Readers are carefully developed by literacy experts to build reading stamina and move students toward fluency by combining standards-based content with developmentally appropriate text.

Level 1 provides the most support through repetition of high-frequency words, light text, predictable sentence patterns, and strong visual support.

Level 2 offers early readers a bit more challenge through varied sentences, increased text load, and text-supportive special features.

Level 3 advances early-fluent readers toward fluency through increased text load, less reliance on photos, advancing concepts, longer sentences, and more complex special features.

★ **Blastoff! Universe**

Reading Level

Blastoff! Beginners — Grade K

Blastoff! Readers — Grades 1–3

Blastoff! Discovery — Grade 4

This edition first published in 2021 by Bellwether Media, Inc.

No part of this publication may be reproduced in whole or in part without written permission of the publisher. For information regarding permission, write to Bellwether Media, Inc., Attention: Permissions Department, 6012 Blue Circle Drive, Minnetonka, MN 55343.

Library of Congress Cataloging-in-Publication Data

Names: Perish, Patrick, author.
Title: Antelope jackrabbits / Patrick Perish.
Description: Minneapolis, MN : Bellwether Media, Inc., 2021. | Series: Blastoff! readers: animals of the desert | Includes bibliographical references and index. | Audience: Ages 5-8 | Audience: Grades K-1 | Summary: "Relevant images match informative text in this introduction to antelope jackrabbits. Intended for students in kindergarten through third grade"-- Provided by publisher.
Identifiers: LCCN 2019054245 (print) | LCCN 2019054246 (ebook) | ISBN 9781644872192 (library binding) | ISBN 9781618919779 (ebook)
Subjects: LCSH: Rabbits--Arid regions--Juvenile literature.
Classification: LCC QL737.L32 P47 2021 (print) | LCC QL737.L32 (ebook) | DDC 599.32--dc23
LC record available at https://lccn.loc.gov/2019054245
LC ebook record available at https://lccn.loc.gov/2019054246

Editor: Rebecca Sabelko   Designer: Josh Brink

Printed in the United States of America, North Mankato, MN.

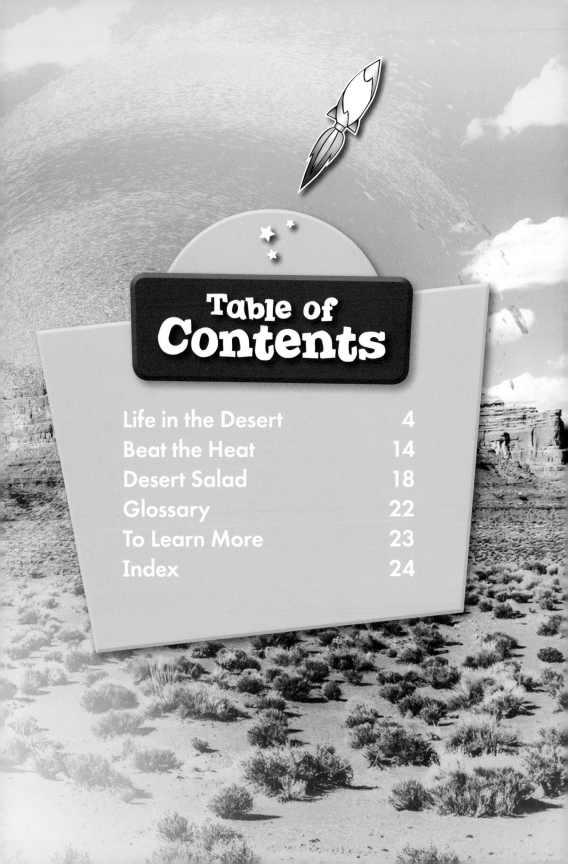

Table of Contents

Antelope jackrabbits live in the deserts of southern Arizona and northwestern Mexico.

These large **hares** are **adapted** to this **biome**.

Antelope Jackrabbit Range

N
W E
S

range = ▢

Antelope jackrabbits have
light-colored fur.

Their fur helps **reflect** the bright desert sun. It keeps the hares cool during the day.

These hares have huge ears! Their ears keep them cool by letting out heat.

Their big ears also let them listen for **predators**.

The desert has many predators.
Antelope jackrabbits are
adapted to escape.

Babies are born covered in fur. Their eyes are open. They are ready to run in a few days!

Antelope jackrabbits have powerful legs. Their legs help them run in a **zigzag** pattern.

This zigzag pattern **confuses** predators.

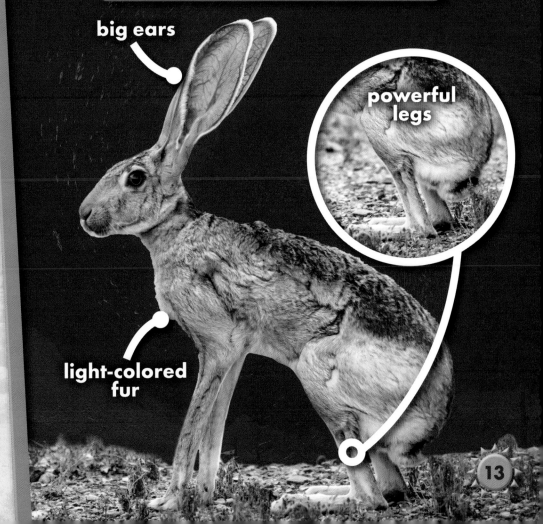

Special Adaptations

big ears

powerful legs

light-colored fur

Beat the Heat

The hot desert cools off at night.

Antelope jackrabbits search for food when **temperatures** drop.

Antelope Jackrabbit Stats

Least Concern	Near Threatened	Vulnerable	Endangered	Critically Endangered	Extinct in the Wild	Extinct

conservation status: least concern

life span: 2 to 5 years

During the day, these hares rest under shrubs. The shade keeps them cool.

It also hides them from predators.

Desert Salad

Antelope jackrabbits are
herbivores. They eat
fresh grasses and leaves.

During dry times, they
eat cacti.

Antelope Jackrabbit Diet

saguaro
cacti

velvet
mesquite

creosote bushes

Antelope jackrabbits get all the water they need from plants.

These hares are adapted to desert life. They are amazing survivors!

Glossary

adapted—well suited due to changes over a long period of time

biome—a large area with certain plants, animals, and weather

confuses—makes something difficult to understand

hares—large, long-eared animals with short tails and powerful hind legs; hares are similar to rabbits.

herbivores—animals that only eat plants

predators—animals that hunt other animals for food

reflect—to throw back heat and light

temperatures—measurements of hot and cold

zigzag—related to moving in a path that has short, sharp turns

To Learn More

AT THE LIBRARY

Cocca, Lisa Colozza. *Desert Animals*. Vero Beach, Fla.:
Rourke Educational Media, 2019.

Eboch, M.M. *Desert Biomes Around the World*. North
Mankato, Minn.: Capstone Press, 2020.

Ridley, Sarah. *Who Ate the Snake?: A Desert Food
Chain*. New York, N.Y.: Crabtree Publishing
Company, 2019.

ON THE WEB

FACTSURFER

Factsurfer.com gives you
a safe, fun way to find
more information.

1. Go to www.factsurfer.com.

2. Enter "antelope jackrabbits" into the search box
   and click 🔍.

3. Select your book cover to see a list
   of related content.

Index

The images in this book are reproduced through the courtesy of: Danita Delmont, front cover (hero), pp. 6, 7; Zack Frank, front cover (background), pp. 2-3; mblanket, pp. 4, 13, 18; Robert Shantz/ Alamy, pp. 8, 16; Rick & Nora Bowers/ Alamy, pp. 9, 12, 17, 22; Hal Beral/ Getty, pp. 10, 20; Paul & Joyce Berquis/ AgeFotoStock, p. 11; Luc Novovitch/ Alamy, pp. 14, 21; Patricio Robles Gil/ SuperStock, p. 15; Nate Hovee, p. 19 (top left); Pritha_EasyArts, p. 19 (top right); Sundry Photography, p. 19 (bottom).